IT'S TIME TO EAT MEATBALL TAQUITOS

It's Time to Eat MEATBALL TAQUITOS

Walter the Educator

Silent King Books
A WhichHead Entertainment Imprint

Copyright © 2024 by Walter the Educator

All rights reserved. No part of this book may be reproduced in any manner whatsoever without written per- mission except in the case of brief quotations embodied in critical articles and reviews.

First Printing, 2024

Disclaimer

This book is a literary work; the story is not about specific persons, locations, situations, and/or circumstances unless mentioned in a historical context. Any resemblance to real persons, locations, situations, and/or circumstances is coincidental. This book is for entertainment and informational purposes only. The author and publisher offer this information without warranties expressed or implied. No matter the grounds, neither the author nor the publisher will be accountable for any losses, injuries, or other damages caused by the reader's use of this book. The use of this book acknowledges an understanding and acceptance of this disclaimer.

It's Time to Eat MEATBALL TAQUITOS is a collectible early learning book by Walter the Educator suitable for all ages belonging to Walter the Educator's Time to Eat Book Series. Collect more books at WaltertheEducator.com

USE THE EXTRA SPACE TO TAKE NOTES AND DOCUMENT YOUR MEMORIES

MEATBALL TAQUITOS

The clock goes tick, the clock goes tock,

It's Time to Eat
Meatball Taquitos

It's time to eat, let's take a walk!

In the kitchen, smells so sweet,

It's time for Meatball Taquitos to eat!

Roll them up with sauce so red,

Cheese inside, they're soft instead.

Warm and crispy, nice and neat,

Oh, how yummy, they're such a treat!

Meatballs inside, all round and small,

Wrapped up tight, they won't fall!

In the oven, they will bake,

Until they're ready for us to take.

Golden brown and oh so hot,

Let's take a bite, oh, what a lot!

With a little salsa on the side,

Dip it in and take a ride!

It's Time to Eat
Meatball Taquitos

Meatball Taquitos, oh so neat,

They're crunchy, tasty, quite the feat!

Each little bite, such a delight,

We'll eat them all with all our might.

Melted cheese and tender meat,

Wrapped together, what a treat!

In the kitchen, we all cheer,

Meatball Taquitos, let's get near!

Bite and munch, crunch, crunch, crunch,

Dip and munch, it's lunch, lunch, lunch!

Taste so good, let's eat some more,

Meatball Taquitos, we adore!

Sharing with friends or family too,

A tasty meal that's fun to chew.

Everyone smiles, no one's shy,

It's Time to Eat
Meatball Taquitos

Meatball Taquitos make us fly high!

So when you hear that clock go tick,

And smell the Taquitos, they're the pick!

It's time to eat, there's no debate,

Meatball Taquitos on the plate!

Let's all sit and eat today,

Meatball Taquitos in a happy way!

Yummy and fun, they're just the best,

It's Time to Eat
Meatball Taquitos

Now it's time for our Taquito fest!

ABOUT THE CREATOR

Walter the Educator is one of the pseudonyms for Walter Anderson. Formally educated in Chemistry, Business, and Education, he is an educator, an author, a diverse entrepreneur, and he is the son of a disabled war veteran.
"Walter the Educator" shares his time between educating and creating. He holds interests and owns several creative projects that entertain, enlighten, enhance, and educate, hoping to inspire and motivate you. Follow, find new works, and stay up to date with Walter the Educator™

at WaltertheEducator.com

www.ingramcontent.com/pod-product-compliance
Lightning Source LLC
LaVergne TN
LVHW052013060526
838201LV00059B/4009